# Drawing
# Barrel Racers
## and Other
## Speedy Horses

by Rae Young

CAPSTONE PRESS
a capstone imprint

Snap Books are published by Capstone Press,
1710 Roe Crest Drive, North Mankato, Minnesota 56003
www.capstonepub.com

**Library of Congress Cataloging-in-Publication Data**
Young, Rae.
  Drawing barrel racers and other speedy horses / by Rae Young ; illustrated by Q2A Media.
     pages cm — (Snap books. Drawing horses)
  Summary: "Step-by-step guides show how to draw a variety of horses and ponies"—Provided by publisher.
  ISBN 978-1-4765-3994-2 (library binding)
  ISBN 978-1-4765-6048-9 (eBook PDF)
1.  Horses in art—Juvenile literature. 2.  Barrel racing—Juvenile literature.  I. Q2A Media (Firm), illustrator. II. Title.
  NC783.8.H65Y67643 2014
  743.6'96655—dc23                                    2013031802

**Editorial Credits**
Mari Bolte, editor; Lori Bye, designer; Jennifer Walker, production specialist

**Photo Credits**
All illustrations are by Q2AMedia Services Private Ltd, except for June Brigman, 28-29, 30-31

Printed in China by Nordica.
1013/CA21301921
092013     007745NORDS14

# TABLE OF CONTENTS

# GETTING STARTED

Some artists see the world as their canvas. Others see the world as their pasture! If you're a horse lover, grab a pencil and a notebook. Just pick a project and follow the step-by-step instructions. Even if you've never drawn a horse before, the projects in this book will get you started. You'll have everything you need to draw a funny foal or a record-setting racehorse.

Once you've mastered the basics, try giving your art a personal touch. Customize each horse's saddle pad or halter with bright colors and patterns. Add in details like silver conchos or textured leather. Draw accessories such as winter blankets, first-place ribbons, or buckets and brushes. Why not try drawing your friends on a trail ride or galloping across a beach? Don't be afraid to get creative!

# TOOLS OF THE TRADE

**1** Every artist needs something to draw on. Clean white paper is perfect for creating art. Use a drawing pad or a folder to organize your artwork.

**2** Pencils are great for both simple sketches and difficult drawings. Always have one handy!

**3** Finish your drawing with color! Colored pencils, markers, or even paints give your equine art detail and realism.

**4** Want to add more finishing touches? Try outlining and shading your drawings with artist pens.

**5** Don't be afraid of digital art! There are lots of free or inexpensive drawing apps for tablets or smartphones. Apps are a great way to experiment with different tools while on the go.

# TURN AND BURN

Pole bending horses weave in and out of a line of six tall poles. Knocking over a pole disqualifies the horse and rider. The horse with the fastest time wins. Draw this horse dodging the final pole and heading for home.

**Step 1.**

**Step 2.**

**Step 3.**

**Step 4.**

## Tip

This horse is a sabino paint. Sabino horses have a solid body with speckled white patches all over. Their legs are almost always all white.

# POLO PONY

Polo ponies help their riders get close enough to hit the polo ball with a mallet. Ponies must be well trained to pick up on their riders' needs. The polo pony must have a thoroughbred's speed, an Arabian's brain, and a quarter horse's agility.

**Step 1.**

**Step 2.**

### Tip

Don't forget to draw this pony's rider! Polo riders typically wear tall riding boots, white pants, a helmet, a safety vest, and a polo shirt.

**Step 3.**

## FACT

Polo is played in periods called chukkers. Each chukker is seven minutes long. Riders change ponies after each chukker to let them rest.

**Step 4.**

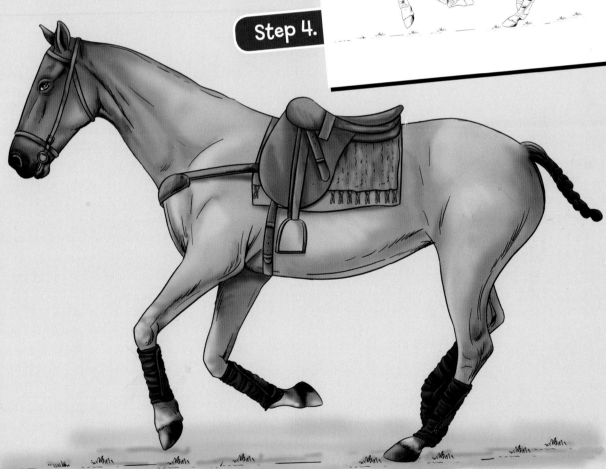

# AND THEY'RE OFF!

Every year in London, England, the Olympia Horse Show hosts a fast and furry event. The Shetland Pony Grand National brings tiny ponies and young riders together.

Step 1.

Step 2.

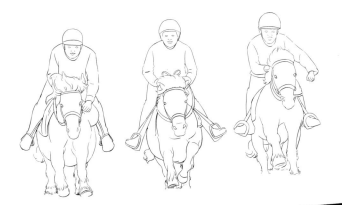

**Step 3.**

## Tip

Pony races are commonly held during fox hunts. Draw adults on their big horses in the background, or foxhounds racing alongside.

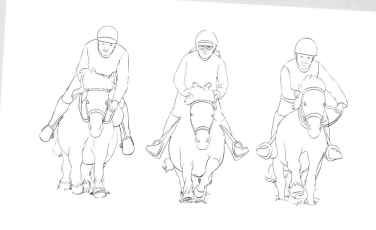

**Step 4.**

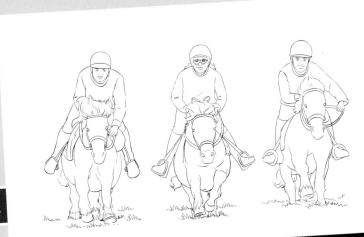

**Step 5.**

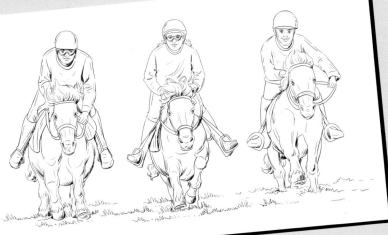

**Step 6.**

# FACT

Riders are divided by age. Ponies are divided by height. Riders must be between 9 and 14 years old. Ponies must be under 42 inches (107 centimeters) tall.

# CART RACE

Thoroughbreds race under saddle. But standardbreds race in harness. They must meet certain speed and time requirements. Standardbreds either trot or pace. This horse is trotting.

**Step 1.**

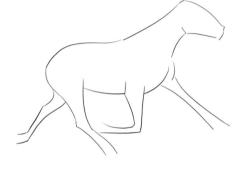

**Step 2.**

## FACT

Off the track standardbreds are thought to be easy to retrain. They are intelligent, calm, and willing riding partners. They have been retrained for a variety of disciplines, including eventing, barrel racing, endurance, competitive trail riding, and ranch work.

## Tip

Trotters, like this horse, move their legs in diagonal pairs. Pacers move their legs in lateral pairs. You can turn this trotter into a pacer easily. Just draw both legs on one side of its body moving forward. The legs on the other side of its body should be moving backward.

**Step 5.**

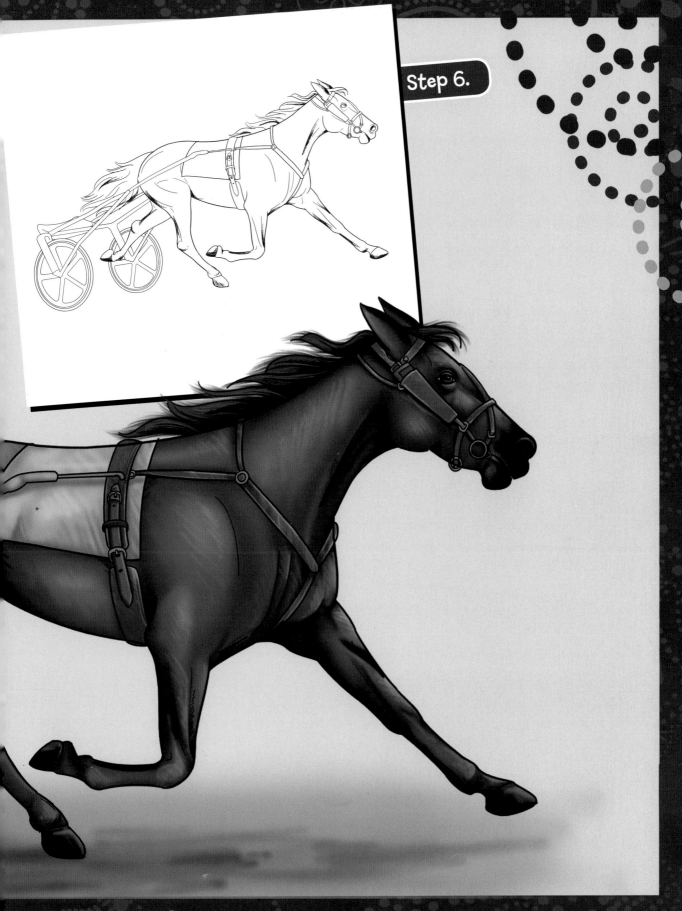

# SLIDING STOP

In 1998 reining became the first Western sport of the United States Equestrian Team. Reining is sometimes called "Western dressage." Reining horses perform patterns at the lope. Each pattern includes eight to 12 movements such as circles, spins, and sliding stops.

**Step 1.**

**Step 2.**

## Tip

Details such as tooled leather, silver accents, and colored conchos can make your reining horse shine. Experiment with different colors, patterns, and styles to find the combination you like best.

Step 3.

Step 4.

# ROUNDING THE BARREL

Barrel racers dash around a course of barrels laid out in a cloverleaf pattern. They race to see who can finish the pattern the fastest. Draw your horse turning the final barrel before galloping for the finish line!

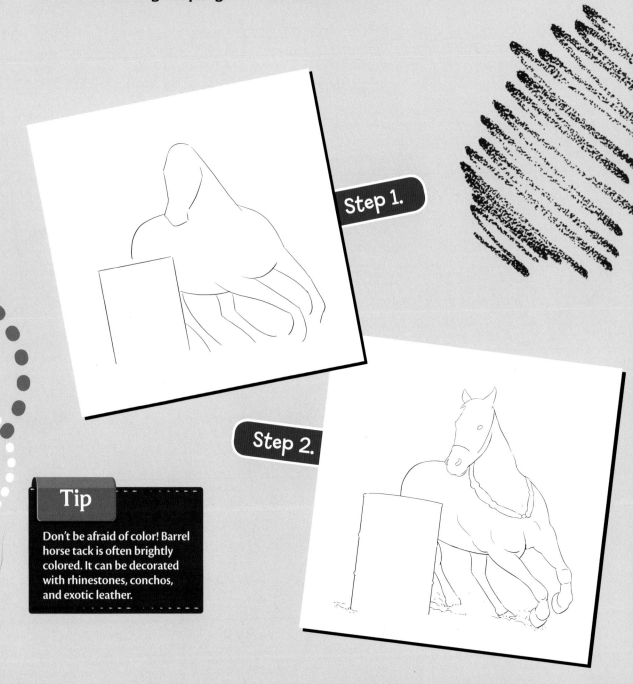

Step 1.

Step 2.

## Tip

Don't be afraid of color! Barrel horse tack is often brightly colored. It can be decorated with rhinestones, conchos, and exotic leather.

Step 3.

Step 4.

# SHIRE FOR HIRE

The average Shire stallion stands 17.2 hands (1.7 meters) high and weighs more than 2,000 pounds (907 kilograms). These giant horses have been described as courageous and forceful. One of the largest horses on record, Sampson, was a Shire. He stood over 21.2 hands (2.2 m) high.

Step 1.

Step 2.

## Tip

Draft horses are shown with long strips of fabric, called mane rolls, braided into their manes. Add seven, nine, or 11 flowers, plumes, or tassels for extra effect. And don't forget to draw a braided tail to match!

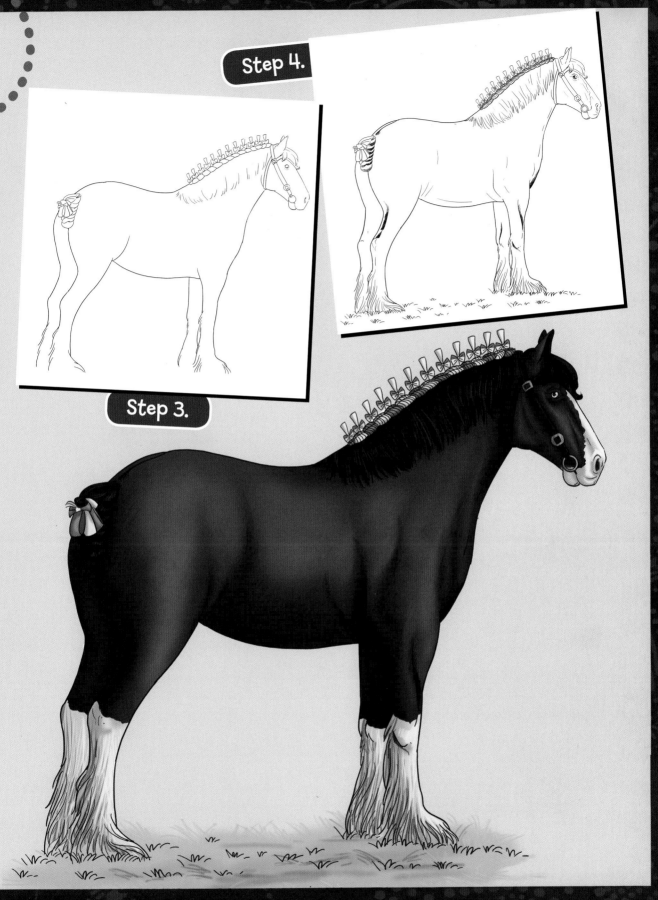

Step 4.

Step 3.

# AT THE TRACK

Pony horses are the hardest-working animals at the track. They accompany racehorses to the track. They also help them warm up, and take them back to the stables after they've run. Give your pony horse a gentle look that could calm any excited racehorse.

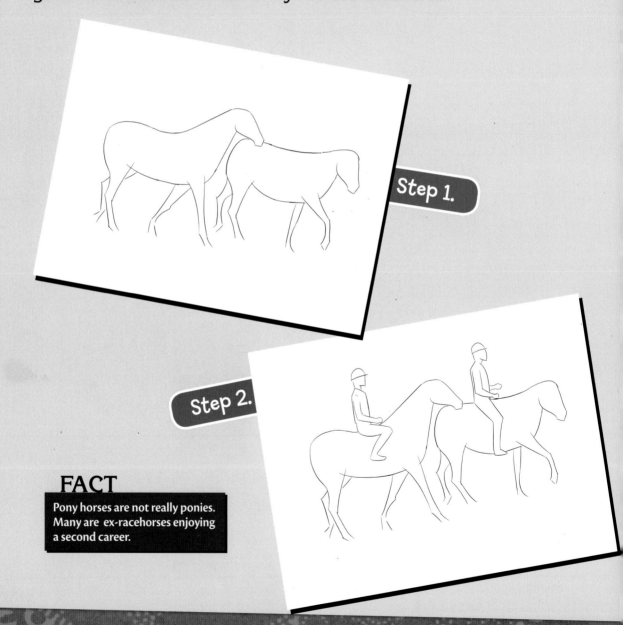

Step 1.

Step 2.

**FACT**

Pony horses are not really ponies. Many are ex-racehorses enjoying a second career.

**Step 3.**

**Step 4.**

**Step 5.**

Step 6.

Step 7.

# HEEL KICK

The image of a bucking horse makes one think of rodeos, cowboys, and the American West. This horse is just getting its kicks while playing in its pasture.

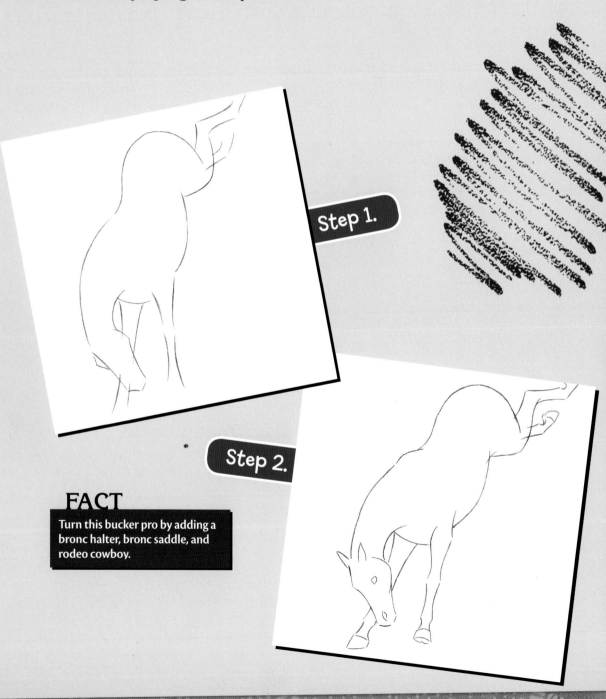

Step 1.

Step 2.

## FACT
Turn this bucker pro by adding a bronc halter, bronc saddle, and rodeo cowboy.

Step 3.

Step 4.

# FLIGHTY FOAL

Foals can stand within an hour of being born.
Strong, healthy foals love to test out their new
legs and explore!

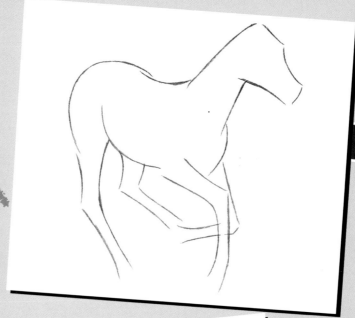

**Step 1.**

**Step 2.**

**Step 3.**

**Step 4.**

## FACT

A baby horse is called a foal.
Male foals are called colts.
Female foals are called fillies.
Colts become stallions or
geldings. Fillies become mares.

# INTERNET SITES

FactHound offers a safe, fun way to find Internet sites related to this book. All of the sites on FactHound have been researched by our staff.

Here's all you do:

Visit **www.facthound.com**

Type in this code: 9781476539942

 **Super-cool stuff!** Check out projects, games and lots more at **www.capstonekids.com**

# LOOK FOR ALL THE BOOKS IN THIS SERIES

**Drawing Appaloosas and Other Handsome Horses**

**Drawing Friesians and Other Beautiful Horses**

**Drawing Arabians and Other Amazing Horses**

**Drawing Mustangs and Other Wild Horses**

**Drawing Barrel Racers and Other Speedy Horses**

**Drawing Thoroughbreds and Other Elegant Horses**